A Congress WBN Publication

Produced By:

 and

DISCOVERING God TOGETHER

Discovery Workbook #5

THIS BOOK BELONGS TO:
_____

About the WE MAGNIFY YOU Discovery Workbook Series

Our families are at the core of our Kingdom Communities. The WE MAGNIFY YOU album provides us with a wonderful opportunity to develop and strengthen the expression of worship in our homes.

Each We Magnify You Discovery Workbook has been designed for parents, guardians, teachers and children to experience and explore the songs together.

Discover new sight of what it means to magnify, exalt and praise our God. Together, our families will develop a deeper and stronger understanding of who God is, releasing a whole-hearted expression of worship unto Him.

For each song on the WE MAGNIFY YOU album, we have a Workbook with the lyrics and specially created activities.

Enjoy taking time together to consider what the lyrics mean. Explore scripture verses that tell us more about each song. Engage in fun activities, including word puzzles and coloring games.

Through it all we can together gain a deeper understanding of how the words we sing reflect the lives we must live, as we align ourselves to God.

Now that is a beautiful thing!

Guidance for Parents

The WE MAGNIFY YOU worship album from Congress MusicFactory contains prayers and songs from Dr. Woodroffe and saints from Elijah Centre and Kingdom Communities across Congress WBN.

WE MAGNIFY YOU is a powerful expression of worship and praise to our Lord. Each workbook in the We Magnify You Discovery Series explores the lyrics of the songs, sharing explanations, key scriptures and fun activities.

These resources will help us to align our lives, our families and our communities to the words that we lift unto God.

BEHOLD THE LORD

LYRICS

Behold the Lord on His throne
King of Kings and Lord of Lords
For His Kingdom is everlasting
His power and majesty endure

We magnify You
Place none before You
We glorify and bless Your Holy Name
Behold Your honor
Your saints together
Offering to You the highest praise

Behold He reigns forevermore
Glorious One whom we adore
From age to age unchanging
Who was and is and is to come

Behold the Lamb, Son of God
Conquering King and Lord of all
Sound Your trumpets, judge the nations
Let all know the Lord Almighty reigns

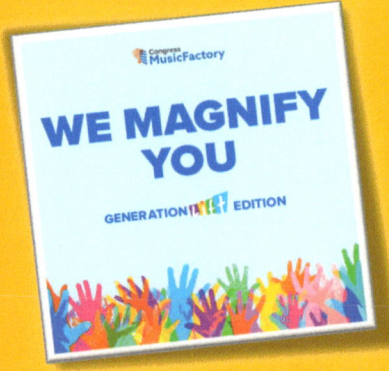

Read, color and learn the verse below:

God rules over the nations. He is seated on His holy throne.
Psalm 47 v 8

BOOK 5: Behold the Lord

A CLOSER LOOK

Behold the Lord on His throne

Behold is like saying, "Wow! Look!"

We are fixing our eyes on something amazing and spectacular, and we want to take it all in!

So, when we say, **"Behold, the Lord on His throne,"** we stop what we are doing and look up at God with respect and wonder. We give Him our fullest attention because He is our King and Lord!

WE MAGNIFY YOU Discovery Workbook Series

King of Kings and Lord of Lords

A king is a leader, like a president or prime minister, who is in charge of a nation.

Our God is not an ordinary king. **God is the King of Kings, and Lord of Lords** - which means He ranks higher than all human rulers.

When we declare this, it reminds us of who's really in charge of EVERYTHING!

Psalm 11:4a says: The Lord is in His holy temple; the Lord is on His heavenly throne.

When we worship we make declarations about the Lord as ruler of all!

Fill in the blanks with the missing words from the song.

> Behold the _____ on His _____
> King of _____ and Lord of _____

Activity Time

BOOK 5: Behold the Lord

The place a king rules is called his kingdom. **God's Kingdom is everlasting** - that means it cannot be destroyed, and it does not get old or fall apart.

His power and majesty endure - we're speaking about a powerful God! He created the universe, our planet and He created man.

His **majesty** is the beauty of God displayed across His creation, from the stars in the sky, to everything in the earth - the birds, the trees, the animals and even the tiniest of creatures. His majesty remains constant and will never fade away!

Write your own words or sentences for each letter of ENDURE, to help you think about what God's enduring and everlasting Kingdom means.

E
N
D
U
R
E

Your Kingdom is a Kingdom that will last forever. Your rule will continue for all time to come.
Psalm 145:13a

A CLOSER LOOK

Behold He reigns forevermore

Did you remember that **behold** means to stop and look, in amazement and wonder?

As we **behold** Him, we see that God is the King of Kings, and that He reigns in Heaven and on the earth. He is a great God—He will never stop doing what He does. He is in charge of the heavens and the earth, He is in charge of our lives, and He will **reign forevermore!**

A CLOSER LOOK

Glorious One whom we adore

When something is **glorious** it is beautiful and stunning to look at. God is the **glorious One** the song is talking about.

Adore means to love deeply. When we think of who God is, what He is like, and all He has done, it's easy for us to adore Him.

BOOK 5: Behold the Lord

Think of your family members who lived long before you were born: your parents, your grandparents, your great-grandparents, your great- great- great- great- great- great- grandparents…!

When we think of many generations stretched out over time, we are thinking of **age to age**.

God has always existed and He remains the same; He is **unchanging**. He is the same faithful, powerful God, forever. From before the earth was created, to when your great-great-great-great-great-great grandparents were here… right up to today, God rules!

Who was and is and is to come - He was here yesterday, He is still here today, He will be there tomorrow, and He will be there beyond the end of time!

WE MAGNIFY YOU Discovery Workbook Series

Activity Time

Match the scrambled words on the LEFT to the correct words on the RIGHT.

Remember to find out what they mean!

HBLDOE	EVERLASTING
OHERNT	GLORIOUS
IGRLSOOU	BEHOLD
DROAE	SAINTS
GIMOKDN	THRONE
LISEAVGRNTE	KINGDOM
IANTSS	TOGETHER
EEHTOGTR	ADORE

A CLOSER LOOK

We magnify You Place none before You

To **magnify** God is to declare that He is the greatest in the whole universe!

When we **magnify** God, we are saying that we make Him the biggest and best thing in our lives.

We **place none before You** means that God is more important than anyone or anything else!

Hmmm... I want God to fill my gaze, like if He was under my **magnify**-ing glass.

Use the clues to solve the crossword puzzle.

ACROSS:
2. Jesus is the ___ of God
4. Blow this to signal the king's arrival
6. King of Kings and Lord of ____
9. Never-ending, like God's Kingdom
12. Rules, e.g. over a Kingdom

DOWN:
1. Who was and is __ ___
3. To last forever, like God's power and majesty
5. The same from age to age
7. God will judge them
8. What we offer to God
10. We bless Your holy ___
11. Behold the Lord on His _____

BOOK 5: Behold the Lord

God's Name is holy!

When we make the right choices, like loving others, being obedient, praying and studying the Word of God, we **bless His Name**!

We can bring dishonor to God if we don't do what He wants or expects us to do. If we are disobedient, dishonest, rude or unkind - then we are not **blessing His Holy Name**.

So, when we sing, **"We glorify and bless your Holy Name,"** we are telling God that we are committed to making the right choices and always living according to His Word and His will for our lives!

A CLOSER LOOK

**Behold your honor
Your saints together
Offering to You the highest praise**

God feels honored when He looks at His **saints together,** reflecting His holy character and nature, obeying His laws, and following His ways. That's us—the body of Christ, singing joyfully and worshipping Him with pure hearts.

We sing, **"Behold Your honor,"** because we understand how marvelous it is for God to see His people, who love each other, all at the same time **offering Him the highest praise!**

BOOK 5: Behold the Lord

Behold the lamb Son of God

In the Old Testament, God's people would sacrifice their best lamb to God to show their love for Him.

Jesus is called the **Lamb**, because He is the sacrifice God Himself made for all of us to be able to know God. Jesus' sacrifice took our sin away - how amazing!

And there's that word again: **behold -** commanding us to watch and observe Jesus the **Lamb, the Son of God.**

Conquering King and Lord of all

A CLOSER LOOK

We know that Jesus is our King and He is loving, and holy and just.

But He is also a warrior and has defeated many armies and enemies who tried to stop His people from advancing. So we say He is a **conquering King!**

A king that **conquers** is one who is victorious in battle.

As God leads us to the Finish, we can be assured that He is able to conquer anything that tries to come against Him and the completion of His purpose.

He is **Lord of all!**

A CLOSER LOOK

Sound your trumpets, judge the nations
Let all know the Lord Almighty reigns

In the Book of Revelation, the sound of trumpets is a signal that God is ready to **judge the nations.**

The **nations** (the countries) of the earth must find out that **the Lord Almighty reigns**. When we obey God and live in His ways, we are bringing judgment to the nations.

Let all know - This is like sending a message to a large group of people - the WHOLE EARTH! It's like sending out an announcement on the Internet, the radio and TV, letting everyone know **the Lord Almighty reigns!**

WE MAGNIFY YOU Discovery Workbook Series

> Take some time to reflect on this song. Here's some space to write down your thoughts.

MY JOURNAL

www.ingramcontent.com/pod-product-compliance
Lightning Source LLC
Chambersburg PA
CBHW041122070526
44584CB00002B/247